The Seven Last Words of Christ

A Bible Study on Jesus' Passion

By Rich Cleveland

Emmaus Journey is an evangelization and discipleship ministry of
The Navigators, an interdenominational religious organization, conducted in and
through Catholic parishes.

The Word Among Us Press
9639 Doctor Perry Road
Ijamsville, Maryland 21754
www.wordamongus.org

ISBN-13: 978-0-932085-98-6
ISBN-10: 0-932085-98-9

Nihil obstat: The Reverend Michael Morgan, Chancellor
Censor Librorum
May 22, 2006

Imprimatur: +Most Reverend Victor Galeone
Bishop of Saint Augustine
May 22, 2006

The Scripture quotations contained herein are from the New Revised Standard Version
Bible: Catholic Edition, copyright © 1989 by the Division of Christian Education of
the National Council of the Churches of Christ in the U.S.A. All rights reserved.
Used with permission.

Made and printed in the United States of America

Cover: Calvary, Andrea Mantegna (1431-1506)
Réunion des Musées Nationaux/Art Resource, NY

To our sons and their wives:

Matthew and Cindy,

Nathan and Lindsay,

and Jonathan and Becky,

who are a constant source

of inspiration and encouragement

to my wife Gail and me.

Table of Contents

Several years ago, while serving as assistant pastor at Holy Apostles Parish in Colorado Springs, I asked Rich Cleveland to prepare a bulletin insert that we could use during Lent to draw people's hearts to the Passion of Jesus. This Bible study is an amplification of those reflections. I commend it to you, both as a personal devotional tool and as material you can use in small faith-sharing groups.

In November 1999, the Bishops of the United States published a pastoral plan for adult formation. In *Our Hearts Were Burning Within Us*, the bishops state: "Adult faith is clearly and explicitly rooted in a *personal relationship with Jesus lived in the Christian community*. . . . Our understanding of the person and the way of Jesus continues to grow by our meditation on the word of God, by prayer and sacrament, by our efforts to follow Jesus' example, and by the sure guidance of the Church's teaching" (55). I believe that this material, which helps us focus on Christ's sacrifice and Passion, will contribute greatly to our ongoing conversion.

In addition, the pastoral plan states: "We encourage all Catholics to spend some time alone with God each day, whether they meditate on Scripture, use printed or memorized prayers, the Liturgy of the Hours, the rosary, meditation and contemplative prayer, or simply dwell in wordless praise in God's loving presence. Even five minutes a day devoted to one's relationship with the Lord can lead to a deepened faith and a more active Christian witness" (110). If you have never established this habit, these reflections by Rich are a good place to begin. If you have established the habit of devoting five minutes or more daily to your relationship with Christ, these reflections will refresh and invigorate your meditation.

Rich joins me in praying that you will be drawn ever closer to Jesus and ever motivated to serve him as you reflect on *The Seven Last Words of Christ*.

Sincerely,
Fr. Brad Noonan, Pastor
St. Patrick's Catholic Church
Colorado Springs, Colorado

Introduction

The Seven Last Words of Christ from the cross, as recorded in the gospels, have been the subject of many traditional devotions and prayers over the centuries, especially for Lent and Holy Week. These seven short sentences, uttered by Jesus as he endured his crucifixion, are filled with significance and meaning. They are both brief and poignant, capturing the depths of Jesus' mercy, physical suffering, emotional torment, and spiritual isolation. If we want to meditate on Christ's experience of the Passion, we can turn to the Master himself as he spoke to those nearest to him and to his Father.

The value and treasure of Scripture is that we have eyewitness accounts of our Redeemer as he lived and died. The gospel writers were inspired by God as they recorded these events, leaving us not only a reliable history of Jesus' life and death but also a window into his heart. As we meditate on all that Christ said and did in Scripture, and especially on what he accomplished through his death and resurrection, our own hearts are filled with love and praise for our Savior.

One of the most fruitful things we can do to grow spiritually is to soak up God's word. Scripture can truly transform us. It is my hope that Scripture will come alive for Catholics using this Bible study and, in the process, bring them ever closer to the heart of Jesus and our heavenly Father. While *The Seven Last Words of Christ* is especially relevant during Lent and Holy Week, when the Church focuses on the events of the Passion, it can also be used at any other time of the year.

The theme for each chapter in this Bible study takes readers beyond Jesus' actual words on the cross to a deeper understanding of what Jesus endured and of the similar challenges and issues we experience in our own lives. In the "Learning from Scripture" sections in each chapter, other stories from the Gospels are explored to find the link between Jesus' words from the cross and his actions during his life on earth. Each chapter features a true story from a Catholic on the topic studied, called

"Experiencing Jesus' Words." A third section includes a prayer, and a fourth section, "Living Jesus' Words," provides questions for further reflection.

As you begin this Bible study, plan on setting aside at least one hour to work through each chapter. (This can be done in one session or in several.) Come with an open heart and mind as you explore the issues raised within these pages: forgiveness, trust, abandonment, obedience, evangelization, and eternal life. As you reflect on Christ's crucifixion, keep in mind that he was victorious over sin and death. His victory is our own. During the course of the Bible study, if the Lord shows you an area in your life that needs changing, be open to change so that you can claim that victory.

This Bible study was developed and field-tested through the Small Christ-ian Communities ministry of Holy Apostles Catholic Church in Colorado Springs, Colorado, so it lends itself to use in small groups. However, it can also be used individually or with a spouse or friend. If you are part of a faith-sharing group, plan on spending another hour or two together discussing your journey. If you are new to a faith-sharing group, here are some helpful attitudes to keep in mind:

1. **Preparation.** The Bible study discussion is built on the premise that each person has invested the time to think about the passages and answer the questions. To be unprepared turns the Bible study discussions into a sharing of opinions. Though you may not be able to prepare every time, to choose not to prepare deprives the group of the blessings of God working in your life. Selecting a specific time to do your study each week and establishing a consistent place to study can help you be prepared.

2. **Teachability.** Try to be open to discover new truths and look at old truths in a new way. We always learn more as we open ourselves up to new concepts.

3. **Wholeheartedness.** There may be days when you feel too emotionally and spiritually down to participate in the Bible study discussion. While it is helpful to acknowledge these feelings, giving in to them can negatively affect the whole group's experience. God can use the discussion and community experiences to lift your spirits. Try to participate enthusiastically even when you don't feel like it.

4. **Willingness to Apply What You've Learned.** The purpose of a Bible study is to change lives, which means changing our attitudes and behaviors. The process of bringing new attitudes and behaviors to life is stifled when we close ourselves off to the attitudes and behavior changes we feel God is asking of us. On the other hand, when we apply the truths we've discovered in the Scriptures, our lives can change dramatically. These will grow into mature values as you continue to follow Christ.

5. **Respect for All Contributions and Contributors to the Discussion.** Each of the members of your group will approach the study from different backgrounds and different ways of thinking. Each person has a valuable contribution to make. It is important to listen and learn from one another.

A special guide is available for leaders of small groups. It includes suggestions for handling the various sessions and for creating and sustaining positive small-group dynamics. This guide can be downloaded for free at www.emmausjourney.org.

May Jesus' words from the cross pierce your heart and mind with love.

Rich Cleveland

Chapter One

"Father, forgive them; for they do not know what they are doing."

Two others also, who were criminals, were led away to be put to death with him. When they came to the place that is called The Skull, they crucified Jesus there with the criminals, one on his right and one on his left. Then Jesus said, **"Father, forgive them; for they do not know what they are doing."** *And they cast lots to divide his clothing. And the people stood by, watching; but the leaders scoffed at him, saying, "He saved others; let him save himself if he is the Messiah of God, his chosen one!" The soldiers also mocked him, coming up and offering him sour wine, and saying, "If you are the King of the Jews, save yourself!" There was also an inscription over him, "This is the King of the Jews."*

(Luke 23:32-38)

For whom does he pray forgiveness? For the leaders of his own people, a fragile, frightened establishment that could not abide the threat of the presence of a love so long delayed. For pitiable Pilate, forever wringing his hands forever soiled. For the soldiers who did the deed, who wielded the whip, who drove the nails, who thrust the spear, it all being but a day's work on foreign assignment, far from home. **And for us he asks forgiveness, for we were there.**
—Richard John Neuhaus, *Death on a Friday Afternoon*, p. 7

Fr. Neuhaus rightly draws attention to our inclusion, both among the guilty standing at the foot of the cross and among those forgiven by Christ from the cross. Sin and its accompanying guilt have been with humankind since the beginning. Someone has jokingly said, "Guilt is the gift that keeps on giving." Unfortunately, never-ending guilt is no joke. It hangs over us like an ever-present cloud blotting out the Son's warmth, where it remains unrecognized, unclaimed, and unforgiven.

Guilt is directly connected to the spiritual condition of our conscience. Our conscience is a witness to ourselves as to whether some action or attitude is wrong. With a little research, we find that the New Testament writers referred to a variety of different spiritual conditions under which our conscience can operate.

Good Conscience—one inclined toward righteous living. (Acts 23:1; 1 Timothy 1:5,19; 1 Peter 3:21)

Weak Conscience—one that is not able to distinguish clearly between right and wrong. (1 Corinthians 8:7)

Seared Conscience—one that is disinclined to righteous living because it has been desensitized by the willingness in the past to ignore inclinations toward righteous living. (1 Timothy 4:2)

Corrupted Conscience—one that is now controlled by false values. (Titus 1:15)

Evil or Guilty Conscience—one whose witness is actively condemning of previous wrong behavior. (Hebrews 10:22)

Cleansed Conscience—one whose awareness that previously unrighteous behavior has been forgiven. (Hebrews 9:14)

Clear Conscience—one whose witness is, "There is no wrong that has not been forgiven." (Acts 24:16; 1 Timothy 3:9; Hebrews 13:18; 1 Peter 3:16)

Our conscience either commends us or condemns us. Regardless of the spiritual condition of our conscience, nearly all of us experience guilt at one time or another. Guilt serves a purpose; it alerts us to the need for forgiveness. If there is no recognition that I am guilty, then there is no conscious need for forgiveness. So as we begin this meditation on Christ's words from the cross, it's important to come face to face with our sin and our guilt as well as Christ's forgiveness.

Looking through the eyes of Christ, we must imagine ourselves standing in the crowd, unwittingly participating in his crucifixion. Because we are not able to bear our guilt, it is crucial to hear ourselves included in Jesus' cry to the Father for our forgiveness. If Christ died on the cross to secure our forgiveness and relieve both the guilt and penalty of our sin, we do him and ourselves a great disservice by not acknowledging his gift of forgiveness and claiming it as our rightful inheritance as his followers.

▶ Learning from Scripture

During his earthly ministry, what did Jesus teach us about sin, guilt, and forgiveness? On one occasion, in response to the Pharisee's accusation that Jesus "welcomes sinners and eats with them" (Luke 15:2), Jesus told three parables: the lost sheep (15:4-7); the lost coin (15:8-10); and the lost son (15:11-32), commonly known as the parable of the prodigal son. Each parable sheds fresh light about the Father's love for sinners and the great lengths to which he goes to find them and bring them home. The parable of the lost son also teaches us about our attempts to deal with our guilt.

1. Let's discover what the parable of the prodigal son (Luke 15:11-32) teaches us about sin, guilt, and forgiveness.

    (a) What were the sins of the younger son?

    _____

    _____

    _____

    _____

    _____

    (b) What evidence does he show that he has identified and accepted responsibility for his sin and guilt?

    _____

    _____

    _____

    _____

    _____

(c) What were the sins of the older son?

_____

_____

_____

_____

_____

(d) What evidence does he show that he had *not* identified and owned his sin and guilt?

_____

_____

_____

_____

_____

(e) Compare and contrast the attitudes of the younger son, the elder son, and the father toward the prodigal's experience.

_____

_____

_____

_____

_____

(f) Sometimes this story is called "the parable of the generous Father." What can we learn about our Father from this story and his desires for us?

_____

_____

_____

_____

_____

2.   The Letter to the Hebrews also speaks about forgiveness. Explain from Hebrews 9:11-15, in your own words, how we obtain forgiveness through Jesus.

_____

_____

_____

_____

_____

Experiencing Jesus' Words, "Father, Forgive Them."

A true story:

When my closest friends betrayed my trust, I became consumed with anger and resentment. Perhaps from someone else, I could have better handled this betrayal, but these friends were committed Christians! Even worse, they had never recognized that they had done anything wrong.

After several months of this smoldering resentment, God enabled me to realize that my anger and unwillingness to forgive were simply keeping their sin alive while also affecting my relationship with him. When I stopped dwelling on their sin and betrayal, I suddenly became aware of my own shortcomings. I began to realize that my sins against the Lord were as bad or worse than my friends' sins against me. As I turned to God for forgiveness, he also granted me the grace to forgive those who had betrayed my trust. For months it required a daily recommitment to receive and give total forgiveness. My friends never apologized, but today they are still my friends because true forgiveness is granted even when the offenders don't understand what they've done.

Praying Jesus' Words, "Father, Forgive Them."

Jesus, those you healed and fed shouted, "Hosanna to the son of David! Blessed is he who comes in the name of the Lord!" Just a few days later, they shouted, "Crucify him!" Your twelve best friends betrayed you, denied you, or abandoned you, leaving you to hang alone on the cross. As waves of pain racked your body, you appealed to the love and compassion of your Father and cried out to him to heal and forgive: "Father, forgive them; for they do not know what they are doing."

Jesus, strengthen me to forgive those who have hurt me. Help me to imagine myself at the foot of the cross, uttering those same words as sincerely and honestly as you did: "Father, forgive them; for they do not know what they are doing." Jesus, allow me to give to others the forgiveness you have given me. By my attitude and actions, allow them to experience your healing love and compassion until they know that both you and I have forgiven them. Help me to live as you died, freely forgiving others.

Living Jesus' Words, "Father, Forgive Them."

1. List those who have hurt you. Pay special attention to those closest to you: spouse, children, parents, brothers, sisters, grandparents, friends, priests, teachers, and doctors.

2. Visualize the face of the person who has hurt or offended you by their words, actions, or attitudes. Tell Jesus about your feelings of anger, resentment, pain, and despair. Ask Jesus to heal you with his love so that you will be able to sincerely and honestly grant your forgiveness to others, as he forgives us when we hurt him.

3. Imagine looking into Jesus' eyes as he hangs on the cross. Continue gazing at him until you are able to join him in saying to the one who hurt you, "Father forgive (name of the person), for they do not know what they have done."

4. See yourself embracing that person with Jesus' healing love and caring arms. Pray honestly and sincerely from your heart that the Father will bless that person's life.

> *God became what by right he was not, so that we might become what by right we are not.*
>
> **Richard John Neuhaus,**
>
> *Death on a Friday Afternoon,* p. 31

Notes for Chapter 1

Notes for Chapter 1

Chapter Two

"Truly I tell you, today you will be with me in Paradise."

Two others also, who were criminals, were led away to be put to death with him. When they came to the place that is called The Skull, they crucified Jesus there with the criminals, one on his right and one on his left. . . . One of the criminals who were hanged there kept deriding him and saying, "Are you not the Messiah? Save yourself and us!" But the other rebuked him, saying, "Do you not fear God, since you are under the same sentence of condemnation? And we indeed have been condemned justly, for we are getting what we deserve for our deeds, but this man has done nothing wrong." Then he said, "Jesus, remember me when you come into your kingdom." He replied, "Truly I tell you, today you will be with me in Paradise."

(Luke 23:32-33,39-43)

*Though there be such things as deathbed conversions, nevertheless as the tree falls, there it lies. One man who led an evil life always boasted of the fact that he needed never worry about his soul when time would end, for he could save it with three words which he quoted in Latin: "Miserere mei Deus." [Lord, have mercy on me.] He was right about saying three words at the moment of his death, but they were not the words he expected to say, for **his life had not been so lived as to pronounce them from his heart.** As his horse threw him over the cliff he said: "Capiat omnia biabolus," which means, "I'll be damned."*
—Bishop Fulton J. Sheen, *On Being Human*, p. 234

When we are young, we seldom think of heaven or are concerned about our eternal future. However, as we approach the latter years of our life and witness life-threatening illnesses and accidents, many of us find ourselves pondering death, dying, and our eternal destiny. "Where will I spend eternity?" is a question that must be reckoned with—and it must be reckoned with on *this* side of eternity.

Contrary to popular belief, our eternal destiny is not determined by a scale weighing our good deeds against the many wrongs we have committed. In this line of thinking, if the good outweighs the bad, we go to heaven, and if the bad outweighs the good, we go to hell. Blessed Pope John XXIII prayed, "When you [Lord] crown our merit, you are crowning your own gifts," and "My merit, your [Christ's] mercy."[1] Pope John Paul II echoed this thought when he reminded us of the teaching from the Second Vatican Council that Christians "owe their distinguished status not to their own merits but to Christ's special grace."[2] Our destiny is dependent on Jesus Christ and his mercy and grace.

Dismas, the thief hanging on a cross next to Jesus, teaches us the true meaning of mercy and grace. We do not know the extent of his sin, but he did, and he accurately judged himself as deserving of death: "We indeed have been condemned justly, for we are getting what we deserve" (Luke 23:41). Aware of his guilt and unable to justify himself in any way, he turned in desperation to the only source of hope available—to a battered, bleeding, apparently helpless self-proclaimed Messiah hanging beside him: "Jesus, remember me when you come into your kingdom" (23:42). With confident assurance, Jesus replied, "Truly, I tell you, today you will be with me in Paradise" (23:43).

Many long for this assurance on their deathbed in the final hours of their life. The lesson of this encounter is that both the mercy and the assurance of our eternal destiny can be ours for the asking. In fact, it is impossible in the Gospels to find an occasion when Jesus ever withheld mercy and grace to those who asked with sincere and repentant hearts.

Do we see ourselves in Dismas? Do we recognize that we too deserve punishment for our unholy deeds? Through Dismas' encounter with Jesus, we can also learn of mercy and grace freely and immediately dispensed to those who ask. There is none so unholy that they cannot come, nor none so holy that they need not come, to freely receive eternal life when they ask from the heart: *Lord, have mercy.*

However, Dismas' last-minute reprieve is not intended to encourage us to put off turning to Jesus for mercy, but to assure us that mercy is ever present and can be received now. Mercy, when understood and received, always produces a spirit of gratitude that results in righteous living.

1. *Journal of a Soul*, Pope John XXIII, p. 274
2. *Mission of the Redeemer*, Encyclical Letter of John Paul II, 11

▶ Learning from Scripture

Jesus' promise of mercy to the thief wasn't the first time that he offered mercy and forgiveness to a sinful person. One illustration of Jesus' grace and mercy at work is the Gospel story of the woman caught in adultery.

1.   Read John 8:2-11 to learn how Jesus used mercy to handle a very concrete and difficult situation.

(a) If you were standing in the crowd observing this scene, what would you be feeling, both before and after Jesus spoke?

_____

_____

_____

_____

_____

(b) What was Jesus *not* saying by his unwillingness to have this woman stoned?

_____

_____

_____

_____

_____

_____

(c) What fosters a spirit of judgmentalism within us?

_____

_____

_____

_____

_____

_____

(d) How would you define mercy based on this incident?

_____

_____

_____

_____

_____

_____

_____

(e) When Jesus says to the woman, "Go your way, and from now on do not sin again" (8:11), what additional aspect of mercy does he introduce?

_____

_____

_____

_____

_____

_____

_____

2. St. Paul speaks about grace and mercy in his Letter to the Ephesians. How does Ephesians 2:4-10 put into perspective both the aspect of freely receiving mercy and the aspect of living righteously?

_____

_____

_____

_____

_____

_____

Experiencing Jesus' Words, "You Will Be with Me in Paradise."

A true story:

Jesus' response to the thief on the cross has been a special encouragement to me. You see, my dad was a lifelong alcoholic. For the few times he remained sober, he was a really nice guy, but for most of my life his sobriety was seldom present. In high school he left us, and we seldom heard from him. In 1986 he died after a lingering illness, alone and estranged from his family. Our family had prayed for him, and had sent him a modern language New Testament before he died. We found it among his meager remaining effects. Did he read it? The worn pages made it seem that he had. Did he believe it? We're not sure.

When I wonder if my dad's in heaven, I can become discouraged. However, Scripture passages like the one about the thief on the cross give me hope that maybe, in the forced sobriety of his last illness, he turned to Christ. If he did, I know that my dad needed to bring nothing more to the cross to obtain mercy than what the thief brought—just himself and his faith in Jesus. This gives me hope that someday I may be reunited with him in paradise.

Praying Jesus' Words, "You Will Be with Me in Paradise."

Jesus, one of your last acts of mercy and compassion was to respond to the request of a thief by opening paradise to him. At the last meal with your twelve disciples, you gave us your body and blood as a way of remembering you and of reminding us that you live within us. You taught us to wash the feet of others as a way of serving you through them. Jesus, show me how I can pass on your mercy to others, especially to my loved ones—perhaps by an affirming and caring word or by a willingness to accept and serve others. Let me recognize and be a vehicle for your mercy, not just in the familiar faces of family and friends but also in the rebellious, the outcast, the lonely, and the needy. Help me to share your mercy and love with others, and let it fuel their hunger for you and for eternal life.

Living Jesus' Words, "You Will Be with Me in Paradise."

Take time this week to engage in a personal dialog with Jesus, and ask him how you can more effectively be an instrument of his love.

1. Ask Jesus to help you discover what it is he has given you to share with others.

2. Ask Jesus to open your eyes, ears, and heart to see and hear the faces and voices of those to whom he wants you to love with his grace and mercy.

3. Allow Jesus to show you when and how to pass on to others those gifts he is asking you to give.

4. Make this demonstration of mercy a way of life.

God is moved by the suffering human heart; the pain of it clouds his face, and we understand who he is and what St. Paul means when he speaks of the "goodness and kindness of God."

Romano Guardini,

The Lord, p. 125

Notes for Chapter 2

Notes for Chapter 2

Chapter Three

*"Woman, here is your son.
...Here is your mother."*

Meanwhile, standing near the cross of Jesus were his mother, and his mother's sister, Mary the wife of Clopas, and Mary Magdalene. When Jesus saw his mother and the disciple whom he loved standing beside her, he said to his mother, **"Woman, here is your son."** *Then he said to the disciple,* **"Here is your mother."** *And from that hour the disciple took her into his own home.*

(John 19:25-27)

In 1938 and 1939, Hitler's persecution of the Jews in Germany had intensified, but mass deportation to concentration camps had not yet begun. However, sensing imminent danger, thousands of Jewish mothers and fathers tearfully kissed their children good-bye, put them on a train headed for England called the *Kindertransport*, and entrusted them to the care of strangers. Many never saw their children again. Later, they themselves would be herded into cattle cars on trains bound for the extermination camps. The heroic decision of these parents meant that thousands of Jewish children would be saved from brutality and death at the hands of the Nazi regime.

As King of the Jews, Jesus did not escape undeserved brutality and death. In addition, he felt spiritually abandoned by his Father. In those final, lonely hours of his Passion, he was rejected by the multitude of people and abandoned by those most dear to him. Once the nails had been driven into his hands and feet and the cross jolted into the hole in the ground, one would think that his pity would have naturally turned inward, but it didn't. As in his life, so in the last hours before his death, his thoughts turned to others—his mother Mary and his disciple John.

How he must have loved his mother Mary, who bore him, nurtured him, and trained him as a Jewish youth! She was the first to witness his deity and power, the first to follow him as a disciple, and the one to stand by him in his agony. John, "the disciple whom Jesus loved" (John 21:20), had followed Jesus throughout his ministry and had returned to stand with him in his final hours.

Theologically, there is much taking place here in this passage: the birth pangs of the Church; and the establishment of a unique familial relationship, not only between Mary and John, but also between Mary and the Church, which John represented.

But humanly speaking, Jesus, Mary, and John were experiencing a terrible tragedy. Not unlike the children of the *Kindertransport*, Mary and John must have felt confusion, fear, grief, and perhaps, too, a sense of abandonment. This turn of events may have contradicted their understanding. They had learned that God was a loving Father, the heavenly Father who had sent Jesus on his earthly mission. Jesus, too, must have agonized over the knowledge that his death would separate him from both his mother and his close friend, even though he knew that his death was necessary for the salvation of the human race.

With the words to Mary, "Woman, here is your son," and to John, "Here is your mother," Jesus releases and entrusts those he loves to the other's care. These final words, delivered in the midst of his Passion, hold special meaning. "The Mother of Christ, who stands at the very center of this mystery . . . is given as mother to every single individual and all mankind."[1] This mystery embraces each individual and all humanity. Consequently, by establishing this new familial relationship in his final hour, Jesus elevated the relationship of Mary to the Church, and the Church to Mary. Faced with death, Jesus entrusted his mother to John's care and his beloved disciple to Mary's care. When we encounter the possibility of separation and death, we can find peace by entrusting the care of our loved ones to Jesus.

1. *Mother of the Redeemer,* Encyclical Letter of John Paul II, 23

▶ Learning from Scripture

A mother's role and influence is extremely significant in the initial development of our character and values. Our mothers also provide an anchor for all we do in life. Jesus entrusted us to Mary, and Mary to us. What can we learn from her in the following two passages?

1. Read Luke 1:26-38, where we first encounter Mary in Luke's Gospel.

    (a) What can we learn about her character and personality from this passage?

    _____

    _____

    _____

    _____

    _____

    (b) From each of the three parts of Mary's response to the angel, what can we learn about following Jesus?

    Here am I,

    _____

    _____

    _____

    _____

    _____

    _____

    the servant of the Lord,

    _____

    _____

_____

_____

_____

_____

let it be to me according to your word.

_____

_____

_____

_____

(c) In your own journey as a disciple of Christ, which of the three statements above cause you the most struggle?

_____

_____

_____

_____

_____

2. Look at how Mary interacted with Jesus in John 2:1-12 at the wedding in Cana.

(a) What does this passage show us about Mary's faith in Jesus and her commitment to follow him?

_____

_____

_____

_____

_____

_____

(b) What does Jesus' response to Mary tell you about his love for her?

_____

_____

_____

_____

_____

_____

Experiencing Jesus' Words, "Here Is Your Son, Here Is Your Mother."

A true story:

I can't completely imagine what was happening emotionally and spiritually between Jesus, Mary, and John as Jesus hung on the cross. And yet, I can, just a little. In my own life, I have had to let go of those whom I love very, very much—my friends, cousins, my favorite uncle, and my mother. Death is a reality. Letting go is a reality. In this way, I am just like Jesus, Mary, and John—we are all born into the intimate and painful process of attachment, separation, loss, and recovery. From birth, I was attached to my mother's love. As I grew up, I had to separate from her, and finally, I had to accept the most difficult separation of all: her death. Remembering her love, wisdom, and kindness helps me to heal. Remembering how she lived tells me that the risen Christ was within her and my dad, giving us Jesus' love. What happened between Jesus, Mary, and John is happening in my family as well.

Praying Jesus' Words, "Here Is Your Son, Here Is Your Mother."

Jesus, you experienced your mother's love from the very first day of your earthly existence until your last breath on the cross. She was ever faithful and true. From the beginning, she was concerned with doing the Father's will and of following you, her son and Redeemer. You explained to those who would listen, "My mother and my brothers are those who hear the word of God and do it" (Luke 8:21). As Pope John Paul II observed, "Is not Mary the first of those who hear the word of God and do it?" (*Mother of the Redeemer*, 20).

Jesus, help me to follow Mary's example of faith, obedience, and love. Many of us have not experienced the love which she showed you, but we praise you that we have been adopted into your family. Through this adoption, may we know your Father, love your Mother, and live in loving unity with our brothers and sisters in Christ. Thank you for being willing to suffer the loss of your loved ones. May we know that you will always share in our grief and feelings of loss when we must separate from those we love.

Living Jesus' Words, "Here Is Your Son, Here Is Your Mother."

Take time to remember and appreciate your natural and spiritual family relationships.

1. Recall and thank God for those who over the years have loved you and helped to form your character and spiritual life.

2. Identify those who have been especially meaningful to you, and thank them for their contribution. Let them know how appreciative you are for all they have done.

3. Make a list of those people whose character and spiritual life you are helping to build up through your words, actions, and deeds.

4. Try to discover one or two things you can do or refrain from doing to encourage others to hear Jesus' words and do them.

> *Mary's maternal function towards mankind in no way obscures or diminishes the unique mediation of Christ, but rather shows its efficacy.*
>
> **Pope John Paul II,**
>
> quoting Vatican II's *Lumen Gentium* in *Mother of the Redeemer,* 22

Notes for Chapter 3

Notes for Chapter 3

Chapter Four

"My God, my God, why have you forsaken me?"

*From noon on, darkness came over the whole land until three in the afternoon. And about three o'clock Jesus cried with a loud voice, "Eli, Eli, lema sabachthani?" that is, **"My God, my God, why have you forsaken me?"** When some of the bystanders heard it, they said, "This man is calling for Elijah." At once one of them ran and got a sponge, filled it with sour wine, put it on a stick and gave it to him to drink. But the others said, "Wait, let us see whether Elijah will come to save him." Then Jesus cried again with a loud voice and breathed his last. At that moment the curtain of the temple was torn in two, from top to bottom. The earth shook, and the rocks were split. The tombs also were opened, and many bodies of the saints who had fallen asleep were raised. After his resurrection they came out of the tombs and entered the holy city and appeared to many. Now when the centurion and those with him, who were keeping watch over Jesus, saw the earthquake and what took place, they were terrified and said, "Truly this man was God's Son!"*

(Matthew 27:45-54)

Appropriately, just before that moment in Jesus' crucifixion when he experienced utter abandonment, darkness descended. Here, as he had throughout his earthly ministry, Jesus was confronted once again with taunts: *"He saved others; he cannot save himself. He is the King of Israel; let him come down from the cross now, and we will believe in him. He trusts in God; let God deliver him now, if he wants to; for he said 'I am God's Son'"* (Matthew 27:42-43). These were not unlike the taunts Satan hurled at him at the beginning of his ministry: *"If you are the Son of God, throw yourself down"* (4:6).

These taunts reveal a favorite tactic of the evil one. During our darkest hour, he tempts us to call into question our Father's will and our Father's love for us. Satan looks for every opportunity to turn life's disappointments into despair. He tries to accomplish this feat by urging us to doubt, in moments of darkness, what God has revealed to us while we were living in the light: namely, the Father's love and care for us. When the evil lies take root in our hearts, we risk falling into discouragement, depression, and despair unless these lies are overcome by the light of truth. The inescapable truth of God's love should become such a reality for us that even when we face a frightening hour of darkness, we should be unable to deny that truth.

We know that Jesus could have called on his power as Emmanuel ("God with us") and saved himself, as he did when the crowd tried to stone him and toss him off the cliff (Luke 4:18-30). That time he passed through their midst unharmed, but this time he chose not to because he had abandoned himself to the Father's will. In the Garden of Gethsemane, he knew that the cup of death awaited him. Though he recoiled from it and asked to be spared from the trial of drinking it, he nevertheless surrendered himself to his Father's will (Matthew 26:39).

As God's Son and our Savior, Jesus hung alone on the cross, with no one to share in drinking the cup of sacrifice and death. He alone willingly accepted the cross and emptied the cup of all the world's sin, including yours and mine. How lonely he must have felt! How complete must have been his sense of abandonment! When he could contain it no longer, he cried to the Father whom he had never forsaken, "My God, my God, why have you forsaken me?" Even in his final hour of darkness, he still did not forsake the Father, but claimed him as his God, crying, *"My God, my God."*

Yet at the very moment of his darkest hour, in the very midst of his utter abandonment, God was there, and he was not silent. In his sorrow at his Son's suffering, at that very moment of his Son's cry, the Father shook the earth and ripped the curtain of the Temple that blocked the entrance into the Holy of Holies from top to bottom (Matthew 27:51). This was God's statement signifying and affirming his love and declaring that the entrance into his presence would forever be open. Now we, in our hour of darkness, need never be alone, need never feel forsaken, need never be in doubt, for God will be there with us also.

▶ Learning from Scripture

Jesus spent the night before his Passion with his disciples, encouraging and strengthening them to face the darkness that loomed ahead. St. John's Gospel records in detail Jesus' final evening with his disciples.

1. Read John 14 to see what we can learn from what Jesus told his disciples.

    (a) How should John 14:1-3 help to quiet our troubled hearts and minds?

    _____

    _____

    _____

    _____

    _____

    _____

(b) What is the hope of the promise Jesus makes to his followers? (John 14:15-18)

_____

_____

_____

_____

_____

_____

(c) How is the peace Jesus promised in John 14:27-31 different from the peace the world offers?

_____

_____

_____

_____

_____

(d) What has been your experience with Jesus' provision of peace?

_____

_____

_____

_____

_____

_____

_____

2.   Read Psalm 22:1-24, which is the psalm Jesus quotes from the cross.

   (a) What additional insights regarding Jesus' Passion does this psalm
       provide?

   _____

   _____

   _____

   _____

   _____

   (b) How can we develop a similar hope in the Father's love, so that
       even in times of suffering our hearts and lips praise him?

   _____

   _____

   _____

   _____

   _____

   _____

Experiencing Jesus' Words, "Why Have You Forsaken Me?"

A true story:

"God, how could this happen?" "Don't you care?" "Now what?"
"What's the use?" "It's hopeless!" These or similar thoughts are indica-
tive of my five-step slide into spiritual defeat: disappointment, doubt, discouragement, depression, despair. For me, this downward descent into
darkness and defeat would happen just before or just after some chal-
lenging situation, when I was most vulnerable emotionally and spiritually and somewhat drained physically and mentally. It always seemed to

happen the same way. Some hope or expectation would be dashed by someone or some uncontrollable circumstance, resulting in deep disappointment.

I've learned to prepare my defenses in advance by reflecting on the permanency of our Father's love and concern. For example, a friend pointed out that I had failed to follow through on several commitments. My first response was to be discouraged about my failures and also to doubt my friend's love and loyalty. Then the Holy Spirit reminded me that God loves me even in my imperfection. To anchor my soul in his love, I've memorized passages like Romans 8:38-39: "For I am convinced that neither death; nor life, nor angels, nor rulers, nor things present, nor things to come, nor powers, nor height, nor depth, nor anything else in all creation, will be able to separate us from the love of God in Christ Jesus our Lord."

Praying Jesus' Words, "Why Have You Forsaken Me?"

Lord, the losses and disappointments in my life often throw me for a loop and cause me to doubt myself, my loved ones and friends, and even your love. Sometimes I feel totally alone and forsaken, as though nobody cared about my dilemma or my feelings. When I am "up" spiritually, I know that these feelings are not based on the truth, but when I am low, I am tempted to believe them. Help me to follow Jesus' example and never forsake the Father, even when I feel forsaken. Help me to ground myself in your love and learn to live in the light of truth rather than in the lies of darkness. Help me to know even in times of loss and disappointment that you *never* forsake me.

Living Jesus' Words, "Why Have You Forsaken Me?"

Disappointment and doubts can be very debilitating for us. However, when we allow the light of Christ to enter our darkness, we will experience release from our feelings of insignificance.

1. Think about how you respond to significant disappointment.

2. Write yourself a letter, as though you were writing to someone who is deeply hurt and doubting, explaining how much God loves and cares for you. Save it so you can refer to it when needed.

3. Jesus is the light of the world. How can you receive more of him into your daily life so that the darkness can be cast out?

4. People who can give you God's perspective when you are going through difficulties might rightly be called light-bearers. Who could be a light-bearer for you the next time you get down spiritually and emotionally?

5. How can you create an environment of light that will call you back to an awareness of the Father's love when you are confronted by moments of darkness?

> *In the heart and spirit and body of a man, God straightened his accounts with sin. That process was contained in the life and death of Jesus Christ.*
> **Romano Guardini,**
> *The Lord,* p. 466

Notes for Chapter 4

Notes for Chapter 4

Notes for Chapter 4

Chapter Five

"I am thirsty."

After this, when Jesus knew that all was now finished, *he said (in order to fulfill the scripture),* **"I am thirsty."** *A jar full of sour wine was standing there. So they put a sponge full of the wine on a branch of hyssop and held it to his mouth. When Jesus had received the wine, he said, "It is finished." Then he bowed his head and gave up his spirit.*

(John 19:28-30)

There is no substance on earth more basic and life-giving than water. We are immersed in water in the womb. Our bodies consist of 98 percent water. And we cannot live without water for more than a brief period of time.

Historically, Roman centurions were not known to be the most gracious of hosts to their captive prisoners. So, it is probably safe to assume that during Jesus' trial, beatings, and the laborious trek to Golgotha lugging the cross on which he was to hang, the centurions were not particularly attentive to Jesus' physical need for water. As he hung on the cross exhausted and depleted of strength, he groaned, "I am thirsty." Imagine! He who said, *Let anyone who is thirsty come to me and let the one who believes in me drink* (John 7:37-38), and he who said, *Those who drink of the water I will give them will never be thirsty* (4:14), now cried out, "I am thirsty."

We have all experienced thirst. Jesus endured a dry mouth and a dehydrated body because he had fully entered into our humanity, with all of its physical needs and limitations. We also thirst at various times, in various ways, and to various degrees, for love, affirmation, and significance. At times, we also may genuinely thirst for God, especially if we have allowed the busyness of life to move us away from him. Eventually we experience the deep spiritual longing of a soul depleted of Living Water. In all the ways that we "thirst," we can identify with the thirst experienced by Jesus.

Was Jesus' thirst simply the physical results of his depleted bodily fluids, or did he thirst for something beyond water? Speaking of this moment, he asked Peter, *Am I not to drink the cup that the Father has given me?* (John 18:11). Could his thirst have been to finish drinking the cup of salvation? Could this cry not reflect his thirst for the souls whom he longed to save by draining the cup of sacrifice?

Fr. Richard John Neuhaus points out: "On the last day of the feast, the great day, Jesus stood and proclaimed, 'If any one thirst, let him come to me and drink.' Jesus is the fountain, and now, on the cross, the fountain thirsts. Reflections on this Fifth Word from the cross traditionally refer to the Church's missionary impulse, an impulse driven by Jesus' thirsting for souls" (*Death on a Friday Afternoon*, p. 145). This hunger and thirst for the salvation of souls was the reason Jesus was sent by the Father from heaven. His thirst to save us was the reason he chose to suffer such an ignoble death.

One attentive soldier offered him sour wine. Perhaps this was a symbol of the world's mocking attempt to satisfy God. The philosophies prevalent in the world often misdiagnose the real source of our thirst and can only offer us sour wine that will never quench our thirst. So when Jesus was offered the sour wine, it did not restore life. He bowed his head and gave up his spirit.

But what will we do with Jesus' cry? Jesus taught that when all the people of the nations were gathered before him, some would be commended for how they satisfied his hunger and thirst. *I was thirsty and you gave me something to drink . . . Lord, when was it that we saw you . . . thirsty and gave you something to drink? . . . Truly I tell you, just as you did it to one of the least of these who are members of my family, you did it to me* (Matthew 25:35,37,40).

Will we mock his thirst by our complacency? Or will we enter into and share in his sufferings, satiating his thirst by embracing his concern for the salvation of souls?

▶ Learning from Scripture

The world is thirsting for living water, and Jesus is thirsting for the opportunity to become the true Living Water for us. He is looking for people who will become conduits for bringing this Living Water to the world.

1. At various times during his public ministry, Jesus spoke of water. Read John 4:1-42 to learn more about quenching spiritual thirst.

    (a) How does this encounter between Jesus and the Samaritan woman demonstrate a twofold meaning of "thirst"?

    _____

    _____

    _____

    _____

    _____

    _____

    (b) To what was Jesus referring when he spoke of quenching the Samaritan woman's thirst?

    _____

    _____

    _____

    _____

    _____

    _____

    (c) What are the attributes of water that would be analogous to Jesus being Living Water?

    _____

    _____

_____

_____

_____

_____

(d) What do you see in this woman's responses that would indicate that her thirst was being quenched?

_____

_____

_____

_____

_____

_____

(e) What can we learn from Jesus' example about making Living Water available to thirsty souls?

_____

_____

_____

_____

_____

_____

(f) How do you feel about being a "thirst quencher"?

_____

_____

_____

_____

_____

_____

2. Jesus' words on living water were reflected in the words of the Old Testament prophet Isaiah. How would you paraphrase the invitation of Isaiah 55:1-4 for people today?

_____

_____

_____

_____

_____

Experiencing Jesus' Words, "I Am Thirsty."

A true story:

As a young person, I felt fairly empty and unhappy inside, although no one would have known it by the smile on my face. I tried finding happiness by doing many good things and by occasionally doing some things that were not so good. But contentment was always elusive and temporal.

One day a Catholic friend began talking to me about God and piqued my interest. Until then, God was hardly a blip on the screen of my life. During the next two years, I was often at the library, reading anything I could find about God. Eventually, I came to understand God's love for me and Jesus' sacrifice on my behalf. As I began to trust and act upon this new understanding of God's love, I was able to tell God in prayer that I desired to follow and obey him. Over time, a peace settled over my soul, and at last my thirst was quenched.

The old emptiness recurs whenever I move away from God, but as I grow in my relationship with him, he satisfies my deepest longings.

Praying Jesus' Words, "I Am Thirsty."

Lord, when I am going through moments of desolation, distress, and loneliness, I need to stop and ask myself, "What am I thirsting for? What am I longing for?" Sometimes I am thirsty for company, the touch of a warm hand, or a friendly word. At other times I may be thirsty for more material possessions, such as a better home or nicer clothes. Sometimes I thirst for righteousness. The question I have to ask is this one: Who or what will I pursue to quench my thirst?

Jesus, when you were dehydrated on the cross—thirsty physically, emotionally, and spiritually—you were offered the world's poor substitute for what you really needed. It could not satisfy you. So when I seek to quench my emotional, physical, and spiritual thirsts, help me not to settle for a poor substitute but rather to seek you, Living Water. Jesus, help me to discern my thirsts and quench them with your comfort, care, and love. Jesus, help me express what I want and need, and look to and cooperate with you to meet those needs. Fill me with yourself.

Living Jesus' Words, "I Am Thirsty."

At his bedside, St. Ignatius of Loyola imagined asking Jesus to be with him and to guide him. As you sit or lie on your bed, ask Jesus to let you know what attitudes, behaviors, and addictions you need to let die. Ask Jesus to be with you through the process of letting them go and dying to them.

1. Imagine yourself with Jesus seated beside you.

2. Share with him the things you thirst for, both the evil and the good.

3. Ask him to help you understand the root of your thirst and to help you thirst only for what is good and right.

4. Ask him to help you learn how to satisfy your desires by drinking deeply of him, the Living Water.

5. Thank Jesus for his promise to help you and to satisfy your deepest needs.

If this Gospel is true, it is not simply "true for me"—it is true for all or it is not true at all.
Richard John Neuhaus,
Death on a Friday Afternoon, p. 156

Notes for Chapter 5

Notes for Chapter 5

Chapter Six

"It is finished."

After this, when Jesus knew that all was now finished, he said (in order to fulfill the scripture), "I am thirsty." A jar full of sour wine was standing there. So they put a sponge full of the wine on a branch of hyssop and held it to his mouth. When Jesus had received the wine, he said , "It is finished." Then he bowed his head and gave up his spirit.

(John 19:28-30)

One can almost imagine the forces of Satan huddled together gleefully, preparing to rush into the field of death as the last seconds tick off the clock. "It is finished" is the message, and they prematurely explode in victorious jubilation, believing that they had defeated the best that God had to offer. But it was only a matter of time until their delight was turned to defeat, for Jesus did not say "I" am finished, but that "it" is finished. His was not a cry of devastation but of triumph, as he brought finality to man's unending search for salvation and freedom from everlasting judgment. Death was destroyed, once and for all.

Listen as Jesus foretold this unparalleled event: *"For this reason the Father loves me, because I lay down my life in order to take it up again. No one takes it from me, but I lay it down of my own accord"* (John 10:17-18) . . . *"And what should I say—'Father, save me from this hour'? No, it is for this reason that I have come to this hour"* (12:27) . . . *"Now is the judgment of this world; now the ruler of this world will be driven out. And I, when I am lifted up from the earth, will draw all people to myself."* He said this to indicate the kind of death he was to die (12:31-33). These three words, "It is finished," referred not simply to the completion of a life but to the completion of judgment. Our debt is paid and the account against us is forever balanced. Nothing need be nor can be added to make forgiveness of sins more complete. It is finished.

Though it is beyond our comprehension to grasp the complex interplay between God's love and God's justice which takes place on the cross, some things are crystal clear. First, there would be no cross were there no divine love. Rightly do we wear a crucifix around our necks and adorn our homes and our churches with this symbol because it commemorates a gift of love. As Jesus said, "No one has greater love than this, to lay down one's life for one's friends" (John 15:13). It was out of love that the Father sacrificed his son. It was out of love that the Son sacrificed his life. And so, ironically, an instrument of death became a beautiful symbol of love, reminding us always of God's affection for us.

Second, there would be no justice without divine sacrifice. Gladly would the Father have chosen some other way, one that was less physically brutal, less emotionally catastrophic, and less spiritually devastating, but there was no other way. The skies were darkened, the earth shook, and the temple veil was torn asunder from top to bottom as the Father expressed his grief. God initiated this great mystery of our salvation primarily because there was no other way he could bring an end to sin and to Satan's reign of terror and death apart from destroying that which he created and loved. There was no other way to declare, "It is finished."

Lastly, while we cannot comprehend the dynamics of so costly a salvation, we can know its effects. Jesus is the atonement for our sins. Our slavery to guilt and shame was broken, and we are now set free from the impending doom that overshadowed our lives due to sin. Our sentence is fully paid. He has procured everlasting pardon for us, erasing sin's record.

Once this truth sinks into our hearts and minds, an unbearable weight is lifted from our shoulders. A sense of freedom engulfs us. Freed from the fear of death and judgment, we are empowered to love God from the heart in deed and in truth. The joy resulting from this newfound relationship with God through Christ overflows into our relationships with people. Appropriating the words of Martin Luther King, we can now sing, *Free at last, free at last, thank God Almighty, we're free at last!*

▶ Learning from Scripture

Jesus revealed more about his impending sacrifice on our behalf as he celebrated the last Passover Feast with his twelve disciples. Let's read John 12:20-36 to find out how he viewed the coming events.

1.   (a) What does the statement in verses 24-25 tell us about Jesus' perspective on life and death?

_____

_____

_____

_____

_____

_____

(b) What was Jesus' understanding and attitude regarding his impending Passion and death?

_____

_____

_____

_____

_____

_____

(c) Jesus referred to himself as the "Light." What does it mean to be "children of the Light"?

_____

_____

_____

_____

_____

2. Isaiah 53:1-9 foretold Jesus' sacrifice on the cross as he described the suffering servant. What new insights about Jesus' sacrifice do you gain from this passage?

_____

_____

_____

_____

_____

_____

3. After reflecting on John 12:24, read Isaiah 53:10-12. How does Isaiah describe the "rich yield" that Jesus' death produced?

_____

_____

_____

_____

_____

Experiencing Jesus' Words, "It Is Finished."

A true story:

It was such a devastating blow when my friend Ruthie discovered that she had breast cancer. She was so young, and she still had two children at home. Initially there was hope, and then came nine years of recurring bouts with the dreaded disease. Ruthie was subjected to just about every kind of experimental drug available. Occasional periods of remission interrupted the continuing spread of the cancer, but finally Ruthie and her husband Bill recognized the inevitable, and Ruthie simply prayed, "Let me live long enough to see my kids graduate from high school." And she did, dying shortly after her last child had graduated.

Enduring the effects of cancer wasn't easy, but for the most part both Ruthie and Bill exuded a love for Christ and a joy for life that, under the circumstances, seemed unreasonable to the observer without faith. It was with relief that Ruthie could whisper, "It is finished." She had completed well the life God had given to her. She finished well, trusting in the mercy and goodness of God, even in the midst of such a painful tragedy.

Praying Jesus' Words, "It Is Finished."

Jesus, at Calvary you had no time or strength left to reflect on your life, ministry, and miracles. The salvation you were sent to procure for us was complete. The battle with sin and Satan was over. In recognition of these facts, as you breathed your last breath, you uttered, "It is finished."

Jesus, you have put me here for a purpose as well. Help me to know how to live in such a way that when my earthly life is completed, I will be able to also say that I have finished the work you sent me to do. Help me to savor the moments you have given me, and to enjoy the family and friends you have brought into my life. Since we never know when the day of our departure from this life might be, help me to express thanks and appreciation each day for all that you have given me. Remove grumbling and complaining from my life, and fill it instead with words of love and gratitude. Help me to give myself to you and to your mission, so that when I depart, I can say with thanksgiving, "It is finished."

Living Jesus' Words, "It Is Finished."

Reflect on where you have been, and are, in your life, and where God wants to take you in the future.

1. Name the people, events, and gifts God has brought into your life. How are they gifts from God to you?

2. How can you express your gratitude to these people and to God for these gifts?

3. What is the purpose or purposes that God wants to accomplish through you? (If you are unsure, ask God to show you his will as you discuss your purpose with a trusted friend or spiritual adviser.)

4. How can you give increased attention to doing God's will and work?

5. Write yourself a letter summarizing what you feel and have learned through this reflection. Seal it in an envelope, and open it in one year as a reminder of what you have discovered.

Love is as strong as death because Christ's love is the very death of death.

Bishop Baldwin of Canterbury,

Liturgy of the Hours IV, p. 76

Notes for Chapter 6

Notes for Chapter 6

Notes for Chapter 6

Chapter Seven

"Father, into your hands
I commend my spirit."

It was now about noon, and darkness came over the whole land until three in the afternoon, while the sun's light failed and the curtain of the temple was torn in two. Then Jesus, crying with a loud voice, said, *"Father, into your hands I commend my spirit."* Having said this, he breathed his last. When the centurion saw what had taken place, he praised God and said, *"Certainly this man was innocent."* And when all the crowds who had gathered there for this spectacle saw what had taken place, they returned home, beating their breasts. But all his acquaintances, including the women who had followed him from Galilee, stood at a distance, watching these things.

(Luke 23:44-49)

Many of us have smiled as we've watched young children hurl themselves from seemingly perilous heights into the waiting arms of their fathers. What a display of complete trust and utter faithfulness! The trust of a child in his father's faithfulness is built over time, based not on the child's ability to weigh the consequences or to evaluate the conditions of survival but simply on the utter dependability and competence of the father to catch and protect. These jumps of freedom begin timidly, and as confidence in the father grows, so grows the child's spirit of abandon.

Jesus similarly left this earth with complete trust in the Father's care, not with a timid whimper of despair but with a loud cry of utter dependence and abandonment to his Father's dependability and care. It was as if he leaped into his Father's arms when he cried, "Father, into your hands I commend my spirit."

At the hour of his death, Jesus was alive with faith. Neither the perilous events of his birth, the threats and disappointments he experienced in his ministry, nor the trauma of crucifixion deterred him from belief in the Father's love or adherence to the Father's will. Jesus' words from the cross are acts of confident faith. Even the "My God, my God, why have you forsaken me?" is recognition that in the face of the horrible separation that was caused by Jesus sacrificially carrying the awful sins of humanity, God was still *his* God.

Jesus the man knew the Father's love. He learned it initially as a child while sitting in the laps of Mary and Joseph as they recounted the miracle of his birth and his deliverance as a child. As a young man, his knowledge of the Father's love increased, and he grew in favor with God and with people. Throughout his life he always did the Father's will, and he always found the Father faithful and his will good. We don't know if or how often the lad Jesus jumped into the arms of Joseph, but through the nurturing of Joseph and Mary, he learned to have confidence and trust in the utterly reliable truth that his heavenly Father would never drop him. And so, at the completion of his earthly mission, he hurled himself with confidence into his Father's arms: "Father, into your hands I commend my spirit."

Due to illness and accidents, we too are sometimes faced with the reality of our mortality. One day we will be faced with the very hour of our death and departure from loved ones. On the day of our death, we too can hurl ourselves with abandon into the Father's arms. This is especially true if during these days of our lives, we develop a similar confidence in God's love and utter reliability. Our daily practice of adhering to his will and seeing his will as "good" is essential to that final act of trust. Hopefully that is one of the truths that we have learned as we have taken this prolonged look at Jesus' final hours and last words.

Jesus died as he lived: forgiving, receiving, caring for others, and cooperating with, adhering to, and trusting in the Father's loving will. These responses were not foreign to him, and he did not need to learn this behavior in his final hours. We too will probably die as we have lived. So the key to dying well later is to learn to live well now, relating to people as Jesus did and developing a living relationship with the Father. Then we will also triumphantly commend our spirit into the Father's hands, and will have confidence in his love and care until the very end of our human lives. Death then will not be an "end," but merely a transition from this human realm to a heavenly one.

▶ Learning from Scripture

None of us will ever suffer as terrible an ordeal as Jesus did, but many of us will experience suffering. Through his sacrifice on the cross, Jesus provides us with the hope to both live and die in triumph, entrusting our life and death to Jesus.

1. Jesus endured suffering and was put to death despite his innocence. The Old Testament Book of Job relates the story of a righteous man who questioned why he was experiencing terrible misfortunate. Read Job 19:1-20 to see how Job described his ordeal.

    (a) What impresses you about his story and to what extent can you identify with him?

    _____

    _____

    _____

    _____

    _____

    _____

    (b) Read Job 19:23-27. In your own words, explain what it was that sustained Job throughout his trial.

    _____

    _____

    _____

    _____

    _____

    _____

2.   Jesus' death and resurrection gives us a hope that the Old Testament writers did not know. First Corinthians 15 elaborates on the resurrection of believers, which is our hope.

(a) What evidence for believing in the resurrection do you find in verses 3-11?

_____

_____

_____

_____

_____

_____

(b) How do verses 42-56 put into perspective a Christian's death and enable us to view it not as an event to dread but as a gift to receive?

_____

_____

_____

_____

_____

_____

3.   Read Acts 7:55-59. Stephen is an ordinary person who fully embraced Jesus' example. To what do you attribute his boldness, faith, and mercy?

_____

_____

_____

_____

_____

Experiencing Jesus' Words, "I Commend My Spirit."

A true story:

What does it mean to commend to God something as holy and profound as our spirit? Pope John Paul II has often spoken about entrusting ourselves to the Lord. These thoughts became very concrete last week as I visited a patient in the hospital who has amyotrophic lateral sclerosis, commonly known as Lou Gerhig's disease. ALS is a progressive disease which systematically causes lack of control over body functions and movement. My friend can no longer move by himself. He is hooked up to a respirator to help him breathe. He can no longer speak. He is completely dependent on others. He commends his body and soul to the care of others. What comes to my mind is how vulnerable and dependent he is.

In reality, though we may not readily admit it, we are all vulnerable and dependent on God. How do we entrust our lives to others and to God? For me, through Scripture and through the action of God in the lives of my friends, I've come to learn of his gracious, powerful, and caring attributes. Through his presence in prayer and in the Eucharist, I've gained an awareness of my dependence on him. At first I learned to entrust myself to him in small ways. Then, as I discovered his dependability, I've come to entrust everything in my life to him.

Praying Jesus' Words, "I Commend My Spirit."

Jesus, it is very uncomfortable to recognize that there is much in life over which I have little or no control. You'd think that as often as I make a mess of things, I'd be more than willing to relinquish control and entrust myself to you, but I don't. I recognize that I have a date with death. It may come in the autumn of my life, or it may come unexpectedly and without warning.

Jesus, I also recognize in your example that there is both a holy way to die well, selflessly and fully cooperating with the Father, and a holy way to live well, selflessly and fully cooperating with the Father. Will you make this a turning point in my life? From now on, I want to dedicate myself to learning from you and following your example. Help me to care for people as you cared for them, to cooperate with the saving mission the Father gave you, and to learn of you and your love. Help me to say now, "Father, into your hands I commend my life," so that when the time comes, I will be able to commend my spirit to you.

Living Jesus' Words, "I Commend My Spirit."

What would it take for you to hurl yourself into the loving arms of the Father?

1. What pieces of evidence are there in your life to indicate either a freedom to abandon yourself into the Father's care or a reticence to give yourself unreservedly to him?

2. What are the fears that prevent you from completely entrusting yourself to God? Write each one of them on a separate piece of paper and describe what you would like God to do with that fear.

3. If God were to remove those fear and anxieties, how would your life be different?

4. Bring each of these fears to God in prayer, whether at your parish church sanctuary, a retreat center, or at a family altar at home. Give each fear to God, asking him to remove it and to replace it with an awareness of some wonderful attribute of his.

5. Dedicate yourself to learning more about the Lord and following his will for your life.

> *He breathed his last not under necessity but voluntarily. His freedom to die demonstrated his power, not his weakness.*
> ## St. Augustine of Hippo

Notes for Chapter 7

Notes for Chapter 7

About the Author

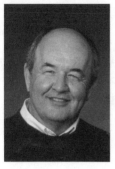

Rich Cleveland and his wife Gail have been involved in ministry since 1974. Rich has served in several leadership positions at Holy Apostles Parish in Colorado Springs, Colorado, including as director of the Small Christian Communities Ministry for the past seven years. He and his wife have three grown children.

Rich also is director of Emmaus Journey: Catholic Small Group Ministry. Through this ministry, Rich and Gail have published several Scripture-based Catholic small group studies. Additionally, Rich publishes *Reflecting on Sunday's Readings*, a small group study based on each Sunday's Mass readings, which can be downloaded for free from the Emmaus Journey Web site at www.emmausjourney.org.

Rich has served as speaker and seminar leader at numerous national Christian conferences and conventions, including the Franciscan University of Steubenville's Men's Conference, the National Council of Catholic Evangelization, and St. Paul's Institute of Evangelical Catholic Ministry.

Also by Rich Cleveland

Learn from Scripture about the way of prayer, conversion, and faith from these Bible studies. The workbook-type format can help individuals seeking to understand Scripture, spouses who want to grow together in their faith, or Bible study groups.

Each Bible Study features:
- Solid Catholic understanding
- Questions for thought or discussion
- Important Scripture passages for each topic
- Plenty of room to write.

Serving the Master
A Bible Study on Stewardship

Serving the Master reminds us of what it means to live out our baptismal vows as Catholics by truly being a eucharistic people. This Bible study explores the practical aspects of being good stewards of our hearts, lives, and mission. Features Scripture passages for study and questions for discussion and reflection.

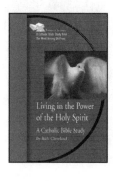

Living in the Power of the Holy Spirit:
A Catholic Bible Study

Who is the Holy Spirit? What is his role in our salvation? How do we receive his fruits and exercise his gifts? These are a few of the questions explored in this nine-week Bible study, which is designed to help Catholics grow in their appreciation of the Holy Spirit and his power to transform their lives in Christ.

Stop by and see us as you journey on the Web

Emmaus Journey: Catholic Evangelization and Discipleship through small groups provides Scripture-based resources and foundational training in Catholic spirituality

On the Emmaus Journey web page, small group studies are *free* to download and reproduce for use in your parish. You will find additional small group resources and free downloads to assist you in your small group ministry.

In addition, at *The Word Among Us* web page, we offer *free of charge* –
- the Scripture readings used at Mass for each day
- daily meditations and reflections based on the Mass readings
- practical articles on Christian living
- reviews of the newest Emmaus Journey Bible Studies

Please visit our websites today!

Emmaus Journey
www.emmausjourney.org
email: info@emmausjourney.org
phone: 719-599-0448

the**WORD**
among us
www.wordamongus.org
email: theresa@wau.org
phone: 800-775-9673